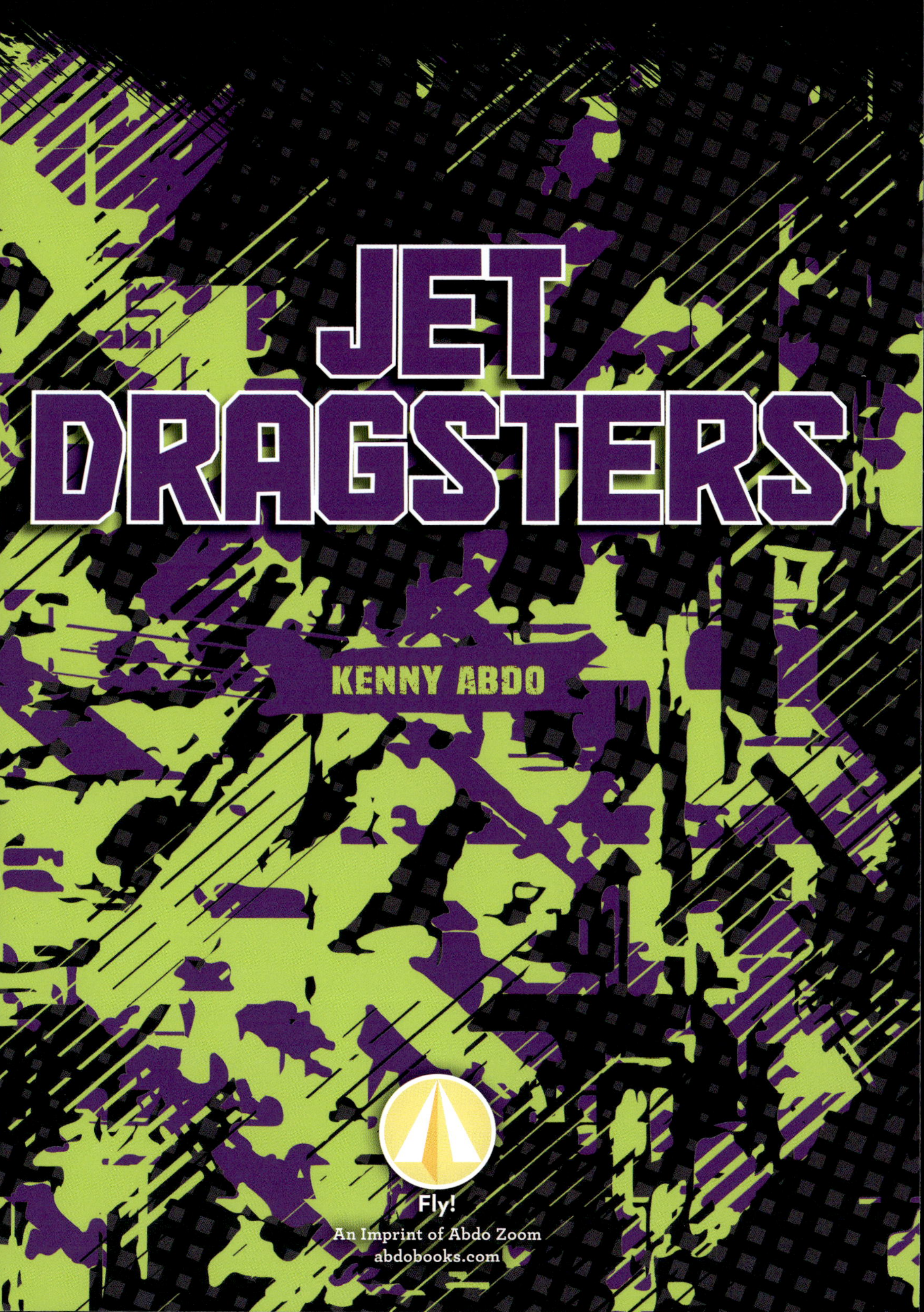

MOTOR MAYHEM
JET DRAGSTERS
KENNY ABDO
Fly!
An Imprint of Abdo Zoom
abdobooks.com

**abdobooks.com**

Published by Abdo Zoom, a division of ABDO, P.O. Box 398166, Minneapolis, Minnesota 55439. Copyright © 2024 by Abdo Consulting Group, Inc. International copyrights reserved in all countries. No part of this book may be reproduced in any form without written permission from the publisher. Fly!™ is a trademark and logo of Abdo Zoom.

Printed in the United States of America, North Mankato, Minnesota.
052023
092023

Photo Credits: Alamy, AP Images, Getty Images, Shutterstock
Production Contributors: Kenny Abdo, Jennie Forsberg, Grace Hansen
Design Contributors: Candice Keimig, Neil Klinepier

**Library of Congress Control Number: 2022946926**

**Publisher's Cataloging-in-Publication Data**

Names: Abdo, Kenny, author.
Title: Jet Dragsters / by Kenny Abdo
Description: Minneapolis, Minnesota : Abdo Zoom, 2024 | Series: Motor mayhem | Includes online resources and index.
Identifiers: ISBN 9781098281441 (lib. bdg.) | ISBN 9781098282141 (ebook) | ISBN 9781098282493 (Read-to-me ebook)
Subjects: LCSH: Automobiles, Racing--Juvenile literature. | Vehicles--Juvenile literature. | Dragsters--Juvenile literature. | Drag racing--Juvenile literature.
Classification: DDC 796.72--dc23

# TABLE OF CONTENTS

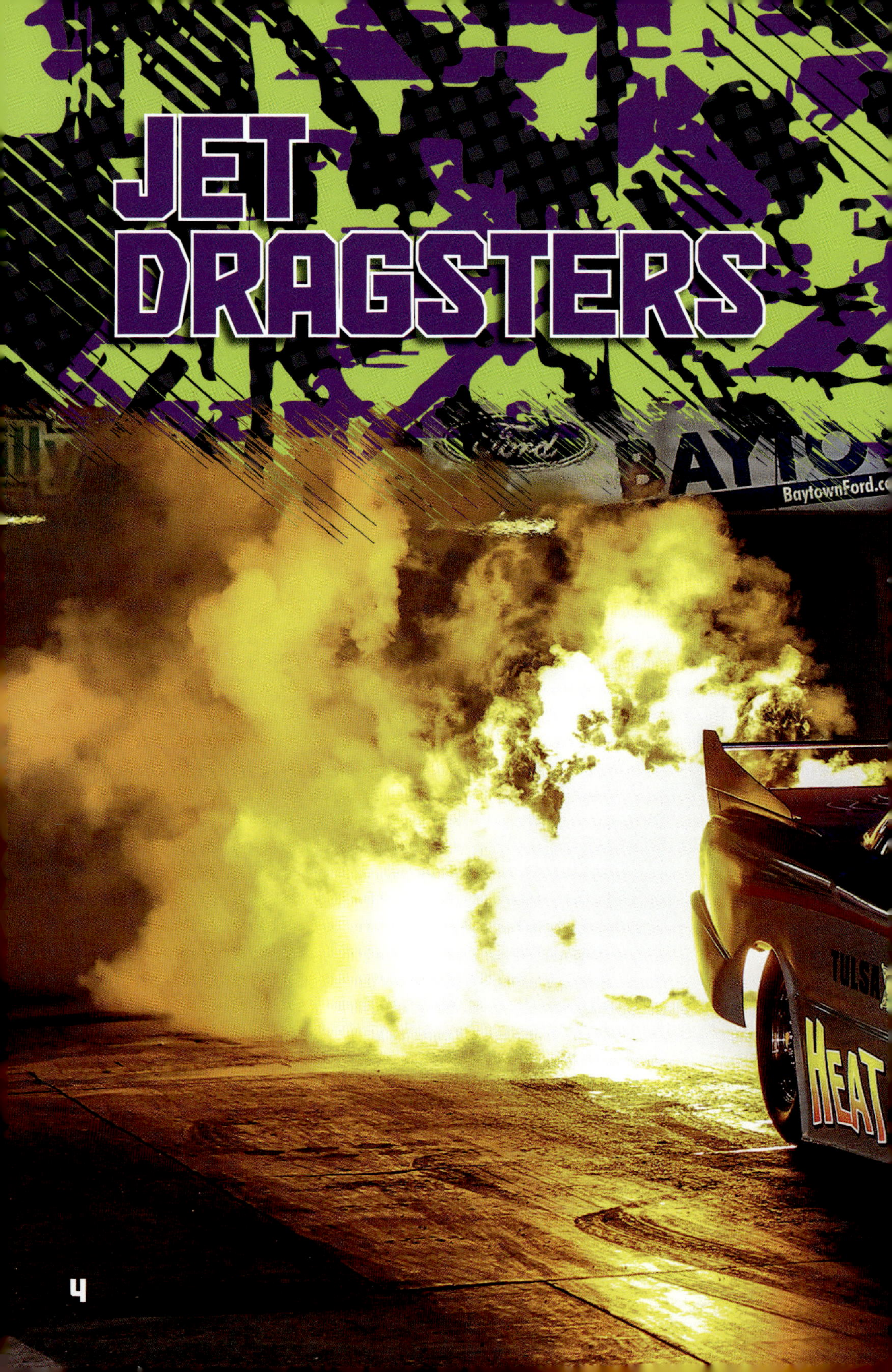
JET DRAGSTERS

Taking what powers an aircraft and strapping them to a car, jet dragsters burn rubber all over other **motorsports**!

Once banned for being too dangerous, jet dragsters have tested maximum speeds and provided incredible thrills.

TOYOTA
CAMPING WORLD
THE ST
LUCAS OIL
NHRA
DEN

# START YOUR ENGINES

The first jet dragsters were built by brothers Art and Walt Arfons. The men had a falling out at the end of 1960. But both were still determined to make the fastest jet car.

SPEED
LIMIT 15
MPH
NATIONAL HOT ROD
DEDICATED TO SAFETY
ASSOCIATION

The National Hot Rod Association (NHRA) thought the cars were too dangerous. So, jet cars were banned in 1961. In 1974, drivers were finally allowed to race the jet engine-powered cars.

# MAYHEM

Jet cars are vehicles with jet engines strapped to the **chassis**. They can reach more than 300 mph (480 kmh) in seconds! The cars use parachutes to slow down to normal speeds and stop safely.

Jet cars are used during drag races. Even though top speed is important, drag races are more about which car **accelerates** the fastest. National jet car races are held **annually** around the country.

E STRIP
LAS VEGAS MOTOR SPEEDWAY
O'Reilly
AUTO PARTS
TOYOTA
Let'
G
DENSO
K&N

SIMPSON
TMS
TITANIUM
@lea

Dragster pilots wear lots of safety equipment, including face masks and full-body suits made of **fireproof** material. They also have fire extinguishers.

Jet dragsters are also used to attempt land speed records. In 1997, a jet dragster reached 763.035 mph (1,228 kmh).

It became the first land vehicle to officially break the **sound barrier**!

BURNOUT
Firestorm
SP Motorsport
Hanna
MOTORSPORTS
DOT7
SPEED

As dangerous as the sport can be, jet
dragsters continue to wow audiences
with their record-breaking speeds.
They will leave tire marks all over the
history of sports!

# GLOSSARY

**acceleration** – the act or process of accelerating or increasing speed.

**annually** – occurring once a year.

**chassis** – the base frame of a motor vehicle.

**fireproof** – difficult or impossible to set on fire or to damage or destroy with fire.

**motorsport** – a sport involving the racing of motor vehicles, like cars and motorcycles.

**sound barrier** – a sudden large increase in aerodynamic drag that occurs as the speed of an aircraft approaches the speed of sound.

# ONLINE RESOURCES

**Booklinks**
**NONFICTION NETWORK**
FREE! ONLINE NONFICTION RESOURCES

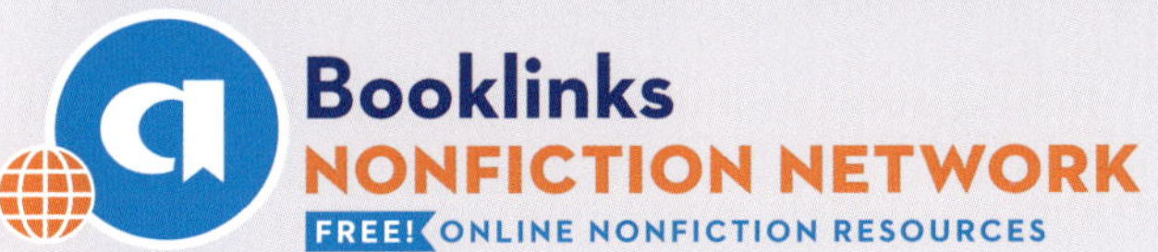

To learn more about jet dragsters, please visit **abdobooklinks.com** or scan this QR code. These links are routinely monitored and updated to provide the most current information available.

# INDEX